CHICAGO PUBLIC LIBRARY
HAROLD WASHINGTON LIBRARY CENTER

Princi

An
Organized Force
for Leadership

DISCARD

Principals: An Organized Force for Leadership

by

Benjamin Epstein

NATIONAL ASSOCIATION OF SECONDARY SCHOOL PRINCIPALS

1904 Association Dr., Reston, Va. 22091

REF
LB
2806
.E78

Cop. 1
Joc.

Copyright 1974

THE NATIONAL ASSOCIATION OF SECONDARY SCHOOL PRINCIPALS
1904 Association Dr., Reston, Va. 22091

ISBN 0-88210-052-1

$2 per copy. Twenty percent discount for 10 or more copies. Special rules for 25 or more copies available upon request. **Payment must accompany orders of $10 or less.**

Contents

Foreword

This past year the Select Committee on Equal Educational Opportunity of the United States Senate issued a report on the role of the school principal. The language of this document left little doubt as to the key leadership role he plays in the school and the community. "In many ways the school principal is the most important and influential individual in any school. He is the person responsible for all the activities that occur in and around the school building. It is his leadership that sets the tone of the school, the climate for learning, the level of professionalism and morale of teachers, and the degree of concern for what students may or may not become. He is the main link between the school and the community, and the way he performs in that capacity largely determines the attitudes of students and parents about the school. If a school is a vibrant, innovative, child-centered place, if it has a reputation for excellence in teaching, if students are performing to the best of their ability, one can almost always point to the principal's leadership as the key to success."

Yet, in their attempts to perform in a manner commensurate with the findings of the report, far too many administrators find themselves literally surrounded by roadblocks. Not the least of these is the hamstringing effect of contracts negotiated between teachers and school boards which fail to recognize the critically important role of the principal. In many cases his individual and professional rights are negotiated away without any semblance of representation or consideration at the bargaining table.

The NASSP has had a deep and continuing interest in both the welfare and professional interests of its members. A meaningful series on negotiations was developed earlier with Benjamin Epstein as one of the contributing authors. At that time he was serving as an assistant superintendent in the Newark, N.J., public schools. With adequate recognition for the secondary school administrator still conspicuous by its absence, it seemed appropriate once again to call upon Mr. Epstein for advice and counsel. *Principals: An Organized Force for Leadership* is the result of his most recent work and we commend its contents to every practicing administrator.

Owen B. Kiernan
NASSP Executive Secretary

Introduction

Why is it that school principals in some cities throughout the nation have affiliated themselves with organized labor within the past few years?

What has happened to make these school administrators, most of whom never thought that they would ever resort to trade union tactics, now vigorously pursue and demand collectively negotiated agreements with their school boards?

What factors have, in less than a decade, impelled principals to organize or participate in local coalitions with supervisors, department chairmen, assistant principals, and central office administrators seeking labor-style contracts spelling out wages, hours, and conditions of work?

How is it that, in the local gatherings of principals across the country, discussions often turn to the wisdom of hiring a professional negotiator, the need for binding arbitration as a final step in grievance machinery for administrators, techniques for formulating a strong set of demands to be put on the bargaining table, lobbying to amend state legislation in order to guarantee the rights of supervisory staffs of school systems to negotiate collectively, or sometimes even the possibility of various forms of "job actions"?

What factors have combined to create the strange contradiction in which principals, who are the key individuals in the instructional management structure in America's schools, have in some districts begun to sound and act less like management and more like organized labor?

Answers to these questions readily emerge from examining and analyzing the multiple traumatic impacts on the principalship during the last decade. They grow out of a period of cataclysmic upheavals, power struggles, embittered confrontations, and continuous crises. Moreover, the effects of the past few years are far from over; they continue to be felt acutely in the schools and press most heavily on the principal.

The purpose here is not merely to review some of the most significant of these impacts or to underscore the toll they are taking in terms of decreased strength and effectiveness of educational leadership and its creative potential in our schools. While it is necessary to take careful stock of the situation, we cannot stop there because we feel that problems somehow will correct themselves spontaneously and without deliberate planned intervention.

What is needed and what principals seek are guidelines for action to change the course of events. With this in mind, we offer in this monograph some practical lines of action for principals and their organizations, local, statewide, and national, to protect and enhance their status, welfare, and—far more important—their continued potential to render maximal service and leadership to their students and schools.

B. Epstein

I. Principals After Teachers' Negotiations

As of 1962, there had not yet been written any true collectively-negotiated agreement between any school board and its teachers anywhere in the country. In fact, not a single state had enacted legislation permitting teachers of public schools to negotiate in good faith and mandating school boards to negotiate. Terms like *bargaining unit*, *mediation*, *fact-finding*, and *binding arbitration* were almost unknown to the great mass of professional educators.

Little more than 12 years later, however, almost two-thirds of all teachers in American public schools are covered by written agreements dealing with almost every phase of the educational structure and process that might possibly affect their welfare and activities in any and all aspects of their employment. By the end of 1971, 27 states and the District of Columbia had operating laws which in one form or another set up a statutory basis for negotiations between teachers and school boards.

Moreover, the non-passage of permissive and regulatory

negotiations laws in the remaining 23 states did not deter the writing of board-teacher agreements in many school districts in a substantial number of these states.

Before the 1960's, work stoppages by teachers were rare and officially frowned upon by the major teacher organizations. But by the early 1970's many thousands of teachers had participated in strikes lasting from one day to many weeks that were taking place in small towns as well as big cities, from Hawaii to Florida. They were conducted under the aegis of affiliates of the National Education Association and the American Federation of Teachers.

During this same period, bargaining units were set up to negotiate written agreements for school nurses, librarians, school clerks, custodians, and food-service workers.

Because principals are the immediate and first line of management in schools, they have to deal directly with the stresses and pressures that emerge from new types of employer-employee relationships.

Antagonistic Staff Relations

One of the sharp changes emerging from teacher unionism is the view of teachers and other employees that the principal is the direct agent of the adversary, namely the school board. This view has been reinforced in school districts where strikes or other strong job actions were undertaken by employee organizations to achieve their ends. At such times principals have been expected by their superintendents and boards to keep schools open, to maintain the functioning of all services, and to keep business going on as usual.

The principal, therefore, becomes the most available target for anger, suspicion, and bitterness in the aftermath of a settlement. Though the principal had little or no part in the decision of employees and board to lock horns in open conflict, he too often ends up as the butt of employee antagonisms—as the voodoo doll into whom the pins of resentment are stuck.

In some communities with strong employee organizations, many principals have been forced to realize that they are no longer regarded as collegial leaders of a mutual educational endeavor, but rather as agents and executives of the adversary ruling establishment. The principal's directives are to be carried out only to, and no more than, the extent required by contract. The principal is reminded, overtly and subtly, that the school staff feels that he will be expected to act as management in any showdown between them and the board. In many schools, principals have to function as the recipients of whatever antagonisms teachers direct at school boards.

Restrictions of Needed Authority

If a principal is to carry out his administrative responsibilities, if he is to organize and coordinate all school activities, and if he is to be responsible for deploying the school staff to educate students most effectively, he must have reasonable authority to make and implement decisions.

Few would deny that the scope of everyday responsibilities has increased tremendously within the past few years. Although one might expect the necessary authority to have been maintained or extended to permit fulfillment of greater performance expectations, the very opposite has occurred. Written agreements negotiated by school boards with teachers and other employees contain a plethora of provisions that many times restrict and reduce the principal's prerogatives. This results from negotiations

—in which principals neither participate nor are consulted—that are based on the expediencies of reaching settlements rather than the protection of educational effectiveness.

Consequently, principals often find themselves hampered in assigning staff members on the basis of competence and training. This is because principals are forced contractually to apply seniority considerations regardless of educational suitability. Professional meetings with a faculty to review operational, curricular, and instructional problems become limited in number and duration regardless of the gravity of the problems.

Flexibility in restructuring school schedules, no matter how valuable or necessary, and experiments with innovations in curriculum or instructional procedures are delayed or totally stymied by arguments that such programs in effect change working conditions, something not to be permitted without negotiations. The procedures for dismissing incapable or incompetent staff members are so complicated and unwieldy that it is sheer frustration to try to move on the subject with any degree of speed. These are but a sampling of contractual provisions that have come to block the administrative effectiveness of principals.

Abuse of Employee Grievance Procedures

It has been held that grievance machinery is a necessary and desirable device to protect employees and to guarantee their contractual rights. But the process can be, and in some situations is, deliberately abused.

The bargaining organization may use it to win continued support of its members, believing that many grievances not only prove the organization's concern for its members but also demonstrate the organization's continued struggle against the school board and its administrators. Grievance after grievance, regardless of validity or merit, is processed in the belief that the organization is obligated to assist every complainer equally.

In most agreements, the principal is the first step in the grievance process. Many principals have discovered regretfully that an employee can easily abuse the grievance procedure. Agreements always protect the grievant from any "reprisals" because he is grieving. For many principals, the grievance process has resulted in either downright harassment or the wasting of valuable hours and energies.

Increased Duties of Principals

A very common outgrowth of the negotiations between teachers and school boards is an increase in the duties and responsibilities of principals—which, in effect, constitute clear-cut changes in their working conditions. What makes such changes singularly unhappy is that, much more frequently than not, the increases in the principal's work load are the result of imposition rather than consultation or negotiation.

For example, many teachers have negotiated their release from a variety of recordkeeping, clerical, patrol, and other duties which they have labelled as non-instructional or non-professional. As a result, these duties have been taken over by non-certificated aids or other paraprofessionals who have been added to the school staff. This development may be a progressive and commendable improvement for reducing the work-load of teachers, but what has it done to the principal? A good measurement in determining the extent of the principal's work-load is the number of adult staff members under his supervision. Obviously, the addition of a number of paraprofessional aids means an increase in the principal's daily work-load.

If a school board were to increase the work-load of teachers without consultation or negotiation with their bargaining unit, the outcry would be loud and angry. Yet this is precisely what at times has been imposed upon the principal. That principals have competently performed under such circumstances does not mean they are any less disturbed or disenchanted by their absence from the deliberations leading to such a change.

II. Do Principals Have Job Security?

The numerous direct and side effects of collective negotiation agreements upon the status and work of principals are far from being the only reasons principals are seeking stronger services from their own professional organizations. At times they may also seek to ally themselves with other administrators and supervisors in local confederations—or to join one of the trade unions within the AFL-CIO, in the hope that such affiliation will yield them more power to protect their status. One of the most deep-seated concerns among principals in many school districts is the inadequacy of job-security protection.

No different from others who work for a livelihood, principals seek a reasonable modicum of protection in the security of their employment. Because job specifications for the principalship today demand extensive professional training, a background of successful experience in education, special certification, a demonstrated capacity and record of leadership, and intense screening during the highly competitive process involved in being selected for the job, principals justly feel that they are entitled to a better level of career security than now prevails in some public school systems.

The Problem of Legal Status

In September 1973, the National Association of Secondary School Principals issued a revised *Legal Memorandum* [1] concerning the Legal Status of the Principal. While noting some gains in the situation since the first report was issued in 1971, it pointed out that in 12 states the school principal ". . . has not attained legal status or identification. He is covered throughout the state code under the general term, *teacher*, with very little or virtually no reference to the principalship as a separate entity."

It also pointed out that, except for 14 states and the District of Columbia, the states ". . . fail to provide the type of legal identification that would provide essential authority and support for the principal in the event of a legal challenge to his rights and responsibilities."

Principals cannot help being driven into restiveness by a system which saddles them with ever-growing responsibilities while not defining their statutory rights in most states to make

---

[1] See annotated listing of all related NASSP publications.

and implement daily decisions. A principal can function only uncertainly when his decision-making power, although board-delegated, is constantly subject to legal challenge on the grounds that it is a usurpation of prerogative not granted by statute.

Because of this same lack, principals in some states have no alternative in negotiations but to be represented by the teachers' bargaining agent, since principals have no separate legal entity. NASSP's *Memorandum* stresses: "This joining together of principals and teachers in many instances has resulted in virtual non-representation for principals." Little imagination is required to visualize what can happen when a crisis of labor relations occurs between a school board and its teachers. The position of a principal, who in conformance with his duties fulfills his management role during a teachers' job action like work stoppage, becomes singularly difficult when he must by law depend for full and proper representation on the self-same organization whose strike he actively helped resist.

What About Job Tenure?

A majority of principals have no rights under law protecting their job tenure in the principalship. Some are employed under the coverage of one-year contracts only. A smaller number are covered by multiple-year contracts. Still others work with continuing contracts—that is, contractual employment continues without formal periodic renewal, but remains nevertheless subject to cancellation at any time regardless of length of service. In some school districts throughout the country, the board of education may arbitrarily demote a principal to teacher status with no reasons given and with no legal requirement for a fair hearing under due process.

Perhaps there is hope in the 1972 action of the Seventh Circuit Court of Appeals. It reversed the decision of a lower court which had upheld the summary dismissal of a school administrator. The Appellate Court said: "A term of employment set by contract has been recognized as a property interest which the state cannot extinguish without conforming to the dictates of procedural due process."

This decision at best brings too little comfort to principals. The length of many employment contracts is too short and they are written in a way that their non-renewal is not subject to challenge.[2] Perhaps it is this general sense of insecurity, more than any other, which makes the protections of collective bargaining agreements increasingly attractive to principals.

The whole problem has become more acute by complex circumstances that have tended to make the principal a special whipping boy in the unresolved ideological conflicts which have torn apart so many Americans and polarized them into hostile camps.

Thus, while one group feels that schools are prison-like institutions seeking rigid, unquestioning conformity and discipline to the point of destroying the intellectual freedom and creativity of youth, a still larger group believes the same schools are centers of loose, libertarian dissoluteness, profligacy, weak moral fiber, with students being reared in an atmosphere that breeds lack of respect for elders, love of country, or law and order. Principals are often placed upon the sacrificial altar, depending on local moods—described as unbending martinets by one camp, as spineless weaklings by another.

Caught in the middle of bitter racial conflicts, the principal

---

[2] See *Employment Contracts for Secondary School Administrators*, published by NASSP in 1974, page 16, for guidelines in contract development.

who tries to be judicious, fair, temperate, and reconciliatory finds himself attacked by both sides as a prejudiced partisan for the other. The principal seems to become entirely responsible for not having prevented confrontations of violence within the school by the very community whose deeply ingrained social pathologies are being acted out in the schools by its children. The community rarely accepts its own guilt; it is much simpler to lay hands on the principal as the scapegoat. "He should have closed the school but he didn't !" Or, "Why did he give in and close the school?" "He suspended too many of our children but always leans over backwards in dealing with *them!*" The conscience of the community is eased when the principal's blood is let.

At hearings before the U.S. Senate's Select Committee on Equal Educational Opportunity,[3] NASSP forcefully testified that, in the process of eliminating the segregation of dual school systems in the South, school consolidations had resulted in wholesale dismissals and demotions of black principals with little or no effort by either state or federal enforcement agencies to protect the job security of black principals on anything remotely near a par of equality with their white counterparts.

NASSP has been no less concerned with developments in major urban centers where many white principals have been egregiously and callously fired or forced out in areas where black or other minority populations have become locally predominant. Such firings commonly are the outcome of highly vocal protestations by self-selected community spokesmen who accuse the principal of a lack of sensitivity or dedicated concern or who insist that only fellow members of their own minority are truly

---

[3] *Equal Educational Opportunity—1971.* Hearings Before the Select Committee on Equal Educational Opportunity of the U.S. Senate, 92nd Congress, Washington, D.C., June 14, 1971.

capable of understanding, relating to, or effectively dealing with the educational problems on hand.

There can be little denial that the previous dearth of black, Puerto Rican, or Chicano administrators in urban school systems is dreary testimony of the long history of deliberate policies of discrimination—in need of drastic and speedy correction. But that the payment for past sins concentrates so heavily on public school principals is grossly unconscionable. Yet, black and white principals, both in the integrating South and the changing Northern urban centers, are the victims. That principals are exploring stronger measures for protecting their careers is small wonder.

III. Concerns of the Principal

The search for better organizational protections for principals is stimulated by the impact of judicial decisions on the administrative practices of schools. When the U.S. Supreme Court, in the celebrated case of *Tinker vs. Des Moines*, established the right of students to express their views on public questions inside schools in peaceful and orderly fashion, the Court fulfilled its role in protecting the constitutional rights of citizens regardless of their age.

The Tinker decision made it clear that school authorities

retained the power to set up and enforce rules and penalties to prevent disruption of the orderly conduct of a school and to protect its safety. Nevertheless, this decision, along with others of similar genre, have increased the range of difficulties faced by principals. Will particular buttons, publications, posters, demonstrations, and club activities lead to disorder or violence? Will forbidding them be adjudicated as violations of the constitutional rights of students?

In NASSP's publication *The Reasonable Exercise of Authority*, Robert Ackerley concluded: "A case-by-case application of these principles will be an extremely difficult, time consuming, and awkward path to follow." And this described precisely what the case is for the school principal; it is one thing to make rulings in the shelter of a courtroom or the offices of a state's chief school officer—it is quite another to be forced to make decisions in the frenetic and volatile atmosphere of a large crowded high school at a moment when it is in the explosive throes of physical confrontations regarding emotion-charged issues.

There is small point in exploring the problem in detail. NASSP has reviewed the area in several publications. It would be a denial of the finest American political and moral ideals and traditions to argue that the rights of individuals, no matter how young they are, may be arbitrarily denied or abused by any school administrator, regardless of the worthiness of his purposes. But it must be emphasized that the limitations resulting from recent decisions of courts and administrative agencies have had a straitening effect on the principal. They unquestionably make his job more trying and troublesome to perform. He has begun increasingly to insist that his professional organizations employ strategies to give his position greater legal support and to broaden his legal powers to carry out his responsibilities.

Bread and Butter Issues

Despite recent improvements in the remuneration of secondary school principals in many school districts, salaries and other benefits have not kept up with the rising cost of living or with the increased work loads and responsibilities of principals Even more disturbing is the wide range of disparity in compensation from district to district, even when such districts are in the same state, subject to identical tax structures and similar fiscal resources.

In March and May of 1973, NASSP and the Elementary School Principals Association published two *Administrative Information Reports* on urban principals' salaries. In addition, ERS, Inc., the research arm of NASSP, completed a comprehensive study of administrative salaries in about 1,600 school districts throughout the country.

These reports reveal considerable disparities. In one New England state, a maximum salary for high school principals in one city was $7,000 per year less than that paid a principal just a few miles away. A comparison of maximum salaries of high school principals in five industrial cities in one of the central states indicated that one city paid its principals from $3,400 up to $5,000 a year less than the other four. Similar dramatic differences occur in one state after another.

An arithmetic average of the maximum annual salaries paid to high school principals in more than 100 of America's largest school districts during the school year of 1972–73 is roughly $23,000. Interestingly, the salaries in 25 percent of these districts are below $20,000. Hence, the average is closer to $18,000. In effect, the principals in 25 percent of the nation's largest school districts earn about $5,000 a year less than what the national average of high school principals' salaries at maximum are. This makes for many dissatisfied individuals.

In addition, examination shows that most principals are on schedules that permit maximum salary only after many years. More than 25 percent of the districts have principals' schedules that take 10 or more years to reach the maximum and some take from 15 to 20 years. Even nine years, which is an approximate average length of high school principals' salary schedules across the nation, is too long—especially when so few school districts offer sufficient security to a principal that he will remain in his position long enough to attain the promised maximum. And as bad as this stretch-out factor is for high school administrators, it is usually worse for elementary, middle, and junior high school personnel.

These same disparities and the lack of prevailing standards are equally glaring in every other area of compensation benefit earned by administrators, be it hospital-medical-surgical protection, dental benefits, life insurance, sick leave, disability, or others that are widely provided to the rank and file as well as management.

In *Management Crisis: A Solution*, published in 1971 by NASSP, an analysis of the basic bread and butter concerns of school administrators is presented. School administrators will find this information beneficial in guiding their efforts to improve the compensation for their labors and responsibilities.

Opportunities to Keep Up to Date

Just as there have been revolutionary upheavals in human relations, economics, and political structures in the span of the last very few years, dynamic and demanding changes have occurred in management procedures; and they are being felt more and more in the structure of American education and in school after school. In each case the principal is expected to administer every innovation as if he were an expert technologist.

Into the linguistics of educational administration have entered terms like PPBS (Planning-Programing-Budgeting Systems); Network Scheduling (including PERT—Program Evaluation and Review Technique); Critical Path Method; computerization (including scheduling, pupil records, computer-assisted instruction, inventory procedures); M.B.O. (management by objectives); and Systems Approaches, M-R (Motivation Research). Similarly, there are arrays of rapidly changing processes, materials, and new ideas in the fields of curriculum, educational resource materials, school building maintenance and construction. The principal who had no such need four years ago may be grappling today with setting up a bilingual program, supervising its operation, and evaluating its effectiveness.

Too few school districts have systematic and deliberately planned programs for on-the-job training activities for their administrative staffs. Neither funds nor time allotments are available to administrators to obtain the training which would return rich dividends to the school system in terms of the principal's increased productivity and efficiency. The computer becomes a threatening monster rather than a tireless, powerful servant.

And this atmosphere of having to cope with the unfamiliar, with no help, or at best some superficial and often confusing hurried orientation, is but another factor contributing to the anxieties and restiveness of school principals and their fellow administrators.

IV. What Can Principals Do?

Most principals experience to some degree the discomforts and discontents that have been discussed. In response they have begun to seek forceful mechanisms and result-producing organizational structures to enhance their security on the job, to fix their legal status on firmer foundations, to give them the authority needed to carry out their responsibilities, and to raise their financial recompense to a level appropriate to the nature of the critical role they perform in education.

Principals have seen teachers, through their organizations, make massive gains in wages, fringe benefits, improved working conditions, and the ability as a group to help shape educational policy; all this has been primarily the result of collective negotiations. Even more impressive is the general recognition that teachers no longer are treated as supplicants. Because of their organizational clout, they now consult and participate in decision making that might affect their welfare or conditions of work.

Not to be overlooked is the increasing number of former leaders of teacher organizations joining the principalship. They have experience as well as the skills in the process, the philosophy, and the strategies of collective bargaining. They are individuals who are not abashed at being described "militant"; rather they find it a posture which they admire rather than reject.

The fact that many school districts have grown considerably in size because of consolidations and population shifts has tended to increase the remoteness of principals from any sense of intimacy with the central office. In addition, there has been a decrease in close person-to-person approaches to making administrative policy decisions, as well as in reliance on personal loyalties. The result is that many administrators feel the need for more substantial protections than a handshake. This has been accentuated by the high degree of mobility among superintendents, which is even greater than that of principals. Principals are beginning to fight for covenants of desirable relationships which, because they have been formalized and committed to writing, have a stability outlasting the tenure of particular personalities.

What Are Some of the Developments?

Principals, along with other administrators and supervisors, have reacted to their anxieties with one universal conclusion—the problems can be resolved only with the help of more action-oriented and aggressive administrator organizations. Very rapidly, principals have increased substantially their dues payments to national, state, and local associations for setting up more comprehensive and service-oriented offices with full-time staffs concerned with problems of state legislation, conduct of litigation to protect principals from improper dismissals, disseminating information on salaries and working conditions, and assisting local units of principals and other administrators in any negotiations they may undertake with their respective school boards.

In several states, coalitions have been formed of school superintendents, secondary principals, elementary principals, and other administrators such as central office staff and department chairmen. Such coalitions, staffed and financed by the combined efforts of the participating associations, serve to unify efforts to influence legislation, to support the development of local functioning management teams, to work with state school-board associations to coordinate and improve procedures for dealing with problems of management policy, and to develop more effective in-service management-education mechanisms.

No national organization has reacted to the changes of the last decade more than the National Association of Secondary School Principals. It has tooled up to give maximum service to its members' needs. A permanent Committee on Status and Welfare was established to review, study, make action recommendations, and set up direct member services. Highly knowledgeable and experienced administrators were employed to devote full-time professional assistance to state and local associations as well as individual members. A number of monographs on problems of negotiations in education, management problems, students' rights, salaries, and fringe benefits were prepared and sent to each member. A full-time legal office was established to do research, give counsel and assistance, and to develop model legislation. In addition, this office has sent NASSP members a series of authoritative legal memoranda during the three years since its establishment. Every convention of the NASSP since 1965 has made available a significant number of discussions and seminars on collective negotiations, bread and butter issues, legislation, and other status and welfare problems. The national staff has promoted and conducted intensive study seminars and institutes for principals on state and regional levels in all parts of the country. Strong and cordial cooperative efforts to deal with common problems have been undertaken with other major national associations of school administrators. Recently, the National Commission on Administrator Relationships was established to assist state and local school district administrators with crisis issues.[4] Representations on behalf of principals' welfare have been made before federal, state, and local agencies. In addition, the NASSP Board of Directors has devoted considerable funds to assisting its state associations in setting up functioning, staffed, self-sufficient state offices.

The trend towards more action-oriented organization has been reflected at the individual school district level as well. At the local level, the formation of administrator and supervisor councils has united the secondary and elementary principals and assistant principals, directors, supervisors, department chairmen, and others. Especially the case in large city school districts, such coalitions result in units large enough to finance the establishment of staffed offices. Their primary function initially has been one of bargaining for the administrative-supervisory staff in local collective negotiations.

In 1970, some large-city coalition units selected representatives to discuss common problems in a series of meetings. They explored the proposition of affiliation with a supervisory national union. They also believed that local units lacked negotiations skills and that they needed professional negotiators to deal with school boards.

---

[4] Members of the Commission are the National Association of Secondary School Principals (NASSP), the American Association of School Administrators (AASA), the American Association of School Personnel Administrators (AASPA), the Association of School Business Officials of the United States and Canada (ASBO), the National Association of Elementary School Principals (NAESP), and the National Council of Administrative Women in Education (NCAWE).

Because of the size of large-city districts, administrators feel distant from their central office and are not willing to rely on management-team arrangements.

And because their bargaining unit is smaller than that of central office and teachers, they feel they need the full strength of organized labor to support their cause. It will give them "muscular clout"—especially in large cities with powerful and influential labor unions.

Too little data exist at present to indicate whether the trend for principals is toward unionization. Neither is it very clear as to what might happen if the demands of the supervisory union and an AFT local were in conflict. I.e., whom will the labor movement support? Or what will the expectations of the labor movement be from the administrator's union in the event of a teachers' work stoppage? As yet, too little experience with this development has been gathered to be able to do much more than speculate or raise questions.

V. Will Administrators Negotiate Collectively?

Whether administrators should seek written, collectively negotiated employer-employee agreements has in some school districts already become a moot question. Such agreements have been written and are in effect in a number of the nation's largest cities, including New York, Washington (D.C.), Cleveland, Baltimore, Newark, Boston, Milwaukee, Detroit, and Portland. On hand in the expanding files of NASSP are copies of scores of such administrator agreements, available for the use of its membership.

In most cases, local agreements are umbrella documents that cover the combined administrative-supervisory staff rather than principals exclusively. This combined staff, as has been noted above, includes principals at all levels, assistant principals, central office directors, supervisors, and coordinators, and in many cases secondary school department chairmen. Excluded from coverage by such agreements are the superintendent and his immediate staff who carry the *superintendent* in their titles, such as deputy, associate, or assistant superintendent.

By definition, the personnel covered by written agreements for supervisor-administrators are individuals who have as one of their key functions the responsibility for evaluating, appraising, or rating other employees. In addition they are empowered to assign and direct the work of such other employees.

There is little point in engaging in hypothetical speculation as to whether principals ought to insist on bargaining for themselves exclusively, or to ally themselves with other administrators and supervisors to form broader bargaining units. The trend towards the all-inclusive unit has been quite definitely established and will, despite a number of difficulties it engenders, probably continue to be maintained—and for several good reasons.

First, the laws of states that permit separate negotiations for the supervisory staff are often written in such language as to clump together into one bargaining unit all staff members of executive and supervisory rank. Second, it is quite likely that any effort to permit separate bargaining by each distinct group in the supervisory staff category would be strenuously resisted by school boards as a costly waste of time and effort, needlessly repetitive. Third, each separate group is relatively small in number, especially as compared with teachers. To the extent that strength lies in unity, larger units lend increased confidence to those who are delegated to negotiate.

The very process of collective negotiations between school boards and their administrative staffs raises a major philosophic question which worries school board members, superintendents, and principals alike. That question, reduced to its simplest basics, asks whether a collective-bargaining relationship between an employer and his executive personnel should exist at all. Unquestionably, negotiations align the negotiating parties into adversary positions.

In daily practice, the principal in each school is the direct representative of the board and superintendent. He is the implementer of their policies relative to teachers, clerks, custodians, parents, students, and the community touched by the school. The principal is the immediate embodiment of the board and superintendent; even the labor agreements made between the board and its teachers and other employees are in the first instance directly administered by the school administrator.

It is felt that principals, playing such a role and given such trust, should at no point be other than integral parts of a total management structure—a structure which cannot be weakened or have its effectiveness diminished by having some of its members in adversary opposition to others.

Proponents of this reasoning tend to think and speak of

principals as members of an administrative or management "team." Contained in this concept is the theme which might be stated as follows: "We the school board members and superintendent recognize and are determined that you, the administrators, and we must work as a tightly-knit integrity in the organization, management, supervision and evaluation of all the elements that must be employed to attain our goal of achieving effective education. We will consult and plan together with you in setting up the policies for our schools. Certainly, such consultation and joint planning will always take place whenever your direct responsibilities are affected. In recognition of our trust in you and our acknowledgement of your critical responsibilities, efforts, and service, we intend to give you such material compensation as your position merits." Unfortunately, this fine-sounding slogan states a schema which is rarely realized in practice.

In large measure, school boards and superintendents operate on the assumption that principals and other administrators can be relied on to carry out directions loyally whether they have been consulted or not. Too often this general attitude pervades the thinking not only of school board members but also of teachers during board-teacher negotiations. Principals, having neither been consulted nor asked to participate, often learn many times too late that their duties and authority as principals have been considerably altered by the new teacher-board agreement. Let it be underscored that even if such alterations improved the lot of principals (which is not the way it happens), the process by which they were arrived at is one in which the school board has in effect permitted a disregard for its administrators—a demeaning of the dignity and status of the principalship. It is an attitude which leads principals to the inevitable conclusion that if they are truly to be management it will come about only as a result of rights guaranteed by a written document.

In districts where the administrative team can and has been made to operate well, where principals do contribute meaningful input into management policy decision making as consultants, experts, critics, and evaluators, the need for a negotiations process still exists. This need has been clearly outlined and described in the NASSP monograph *Management Crisis* mentioned earlier. Such negotiations need not proceed on an adversary basis. Items such as salaries, fringe benefits, sick leave, job security, and vacation provisions can be determined by cooperative study; settlements can be achieved without rancor where confidence in each other's sincerity prevails.

Even the existence and operational structure of the "administrative team" is a valid subject of negotiation. The "team" all too commonly exists and functions well because of particular personalities. It may readily disappear or grow dormant when the persons of the superintendent or board members change. Had the structure, operation, and spheres of responsibility of the "administrative team" been negotiated, formalized into written agreement between the board and its administrators, and officially enacted into the rules governing the operation of the board and superintendent, the "team" would not suffer a possible fate of fragile transiency.

Principals in some districts will find that the protection and improvement of their status and welfare will come about only as a result of collective negotiations. In districts where principals are treated as management, there is a sense of security in written agreements, should attitudes or conditions change in their school system.

Principals should, therefore, work to ensure the existence of state statutes that guarantee their right to negotiate. Such laws should also mandate school boards to negotiate in good faith. Local and state principals' associations should unite with comparable associations for other supervisory staff toward the end of influencing legislation.

Some states have no laws enabling and mandating negotiations for any professionals in education—either teachers or administrators. In these states, efforts should be made to enact effective legislation on collective negotiations; such statutes should include the specific rights of administrative and supervisory personnel to represent their interests as a specific group. Among the states where such action is needed are: Alabama, Arizona, Arkansas, Colorado, Georgia, Illinois, Indiana, Kentucky, Louisiana, Mississippi, Missouri, Montana, New Hampshire, New Mexico, North Carolina, Ohio, Oklahoma, South Carolina, Tennessee, Utah, Virginia, West Virginia, and Wyoming.

In this entire consideration, NASSP's recommendations in *A Legal Memorandum* concerning the Legal Status of the Principal, published September, 1973, are timely and significant. The enactment of laws defining the nature of the principalship and distinguishing it from non-administrative and non-supervisory positions can be a crucial step in establishing the managerial function of the principalship.

In all legislation on the principal's right to negotiate, it is a sine qua non that the school board be mandated to negotiate in good faith. Standards for such good faith must include safeguards against the use of delaying tactics, reprisals for organizational leadership, and the right of administrative employees to enter into negotiations affecting their managerial and supervisory functions.

The strongest hope for improving principals' status and welfare by way of collective negotiations lies in well-written and strongly enforceable state laws. It would be foolhardy for principals and other supervisory staff to believe that they can be effective by resorting to muscle-flexing efforts such as work-stoppages, slow-downs, public demonstrations, and other similar job-actions, or the threat to employ such tactics. The paucity of their numbers as well as the nature of their function reduces any such strategies to a tilting at windmills. Moreover, the use of such devices, most likely, would destroy any trace of confidence by school boards in entrusting management prerogatives to administrators.

Certainly, it is the right of principals to form and join such organizations as they may choose to represent them in negotiations or in any other relationship with their school boards and superintendents. This right should in no way be abridged or judged improper if the organizations are trade unions affiliated with the organized labor movement. But announcing to a school board prior to or during negotiations that, unless negotiations are settled to the satisfaction of the administrative staff, they as a group intend to join or form a union cannot be regarded as other than a threat—as well as an exploitation of organized labor. School boards during the last five to 10 years have become much more sophisticated in such matters; they have developed know-how and experience with negotiations; they have learned to work with and deal cordially and intelligently with many labor unions representing both instructional and now managerial employees; they have heard threats and dealt with crises before and no longer frighten very easily.

Principals should consider one caveat in any of their efforts at collective negotiations. Regardless of the respect and admiration which they may properly have for the effectiveness of organized labor in achieving gains for its membership, if principals wish to be treated as management, with its prerogatives and remunerations, they must employ the strategies of *managerial* employees to secure their goals, rather than those of *rank and file workers*.

Does such a caveat mean, when principals negotiate with their boards and reach the point of impasse, that they are left with no recourse but to accept whatever patronage the board is willing to give—and no more? Not at all !

Negotiations laws should provide for speedy and effective remedies for the resolutions of impasses without public recriminations, accusations by both sides of intractibility, charges of nonconcern, and other acts provoked by charged emotions. Such remedies can be most effective in achieving rational and satisfying acceptance by both school boards and their administrators. They include mediation, fact-finding, and arbitration. It is not the purpose here to explore these techniques of conciliation. However, it might be worth stressing that, if the mediators, fact-finders, and arbitrators are familiar and knowledgeable of public education, their interventions are far more likely to be successful than if their backgrounds are rooted primarily in the experiences of the private sector.

Even when legislation does not provide for adequate remedies to overcome an impasse, it is quite possible and practical for both parties to set up local ground rules for negotiations which include such remedies. One of the possible reasons why school board members and administrators alike have been skeptical about such impasse remedies has been that the recommendations of fact-finders and arbitrators have been advisory rather than binding. As a result, impasses continue if either party refuses to accept the recommendations.

Perhaps the time has arrived for school boards and their administrative staffs to move a step further in order to reach reasonable conclusions more expeditiously. This step would be the mutual acceptance of binding arbitration in impasse resolution using an arbitration panel completely acceptable to both parties. It is possible to visualize a tripartite panel made of (1) a nominee of the administrators coming from another school district selected from the ranks of leadership of a statewide administrators organization, (2) a nominee of the school board also from outside of the school district selected from the membership of the state school board association, and (3) a neutral chairman acceptable to both parties nominated by either the state bar association, the state chamber of commerce, or some similar organization. It is probable that a panel of such caliber could offer a resolution of the impasse, sharing knowledge of the problems of school boards, administrators, and management, and operating with considerateness to both sides of the bargaining table.

If the will to cooperate really saturates the conduct of board-administrator negotiations, ways can be found to reach acceptable settlements without all of these devices. Where adversary attitudes prevail, impasse remedies become a necessity for the board and administrators alike—regardless of the size of a district.

VI. Agenda for Negotiations

What will appear on an agenda for negotiations between principals and school boards depends greatly on the nature of the school district. Obviously, many differences between school districts in terms of size, population make-up, the local community's wealth and economy, as well as local patterns of thinking and traditions, preclude any simple prescriptions about what to include on the agenda. The priority items for the agenda in each school district will be those aimed at the major sources of dissatisfaction, anxiety, and difficulty. While salary considerations may have priority in one community, they may have little significance in another where job security is a major concern.

At least four categories are essential for satisfying the needs and concerns of principals.

The Practical Rewards of the Job

For most principals, salaries must be raised to a norm much higher than the current one. Second, a concerted effort should be undertaken in most districts to reduce the number of years needed to achieve maximum salary to no more than three years.

Third, the tying of principals' salaries to teachers' is unfair to principals, based on a false logic which seeks "not to increase the gap" between administrators' salaries and teachers' salaries. Negotiations of teachers has reduced their work-load, but the pattern for principals has been just the opposite and marked by increased work and responsibility. The increase merits a recompense that should be reflected in salaries and in fringe benefits, sick leave provisions, leave for in-service activities, and disability and life insurance.

While it can hardly be thought of as job remuneration, principals require and deserve adequate insurance for indemnity in costs arising out of civil and criminal actions brought against them as a result of the legitimate performance of their duties. Principals have a high vulnerability to, and are increasingly subject to, all sorts of litigation involving the many areas of their responsibility—from injury on the football field to the disgruntled student turned down for membership in the school's honor society. Principals should not have to reduce their income to cover insurance costs.

Job Security

Justification of any system of long-term tenure for professional educators—teachers as well as administrators—is being heavily debated on the grounds that tenure makes the removal of incompetent individuals unduly difficult.

NASSP's *Legal Memorandum* on the Administrator's Right to Continuing Employment points out that principals who wish to consider themselves management ". . . will have to recognize that their increased status and privileges are likely to be accompanied by the loss of the legal protection afforded to instructional employees." It is unlikely that any effort to attain or strengthen statutory tenure for principals will be successful at the present moment. The collective negotiations process, however, does afford an effective tool for developing a better level of job security than many principals enjoy.

Certainly no job security program should ever protect incompetence, inefficiency, or neglect of duties. It should provide as a minimum:

- An individual contract of employment for at least two years from the initial date of employment.
- Automatic renewal or continuance of employment for at least one year unless reasonable notice of non-reemployment is given—in the case of principals the notice should be a minimum of six months prior to the terminal date of the contract.
- Protection against summary dismissal by guarantees of the rights of the individual to receive a written list of the complaints or charges against him, to full due process including representation by counsel, the presentation of defense, and confrontation of deprecatory witnesses and materials by cross-examination.
- Requirements that superordinate judgments of the competence effectiveness of the principal be made on the basis of more objective and less subjective means of appraisal, such as measurements of the attainment of pre-set performance objectives.

An "Accountability" System

School boards and principals who are currently negotiating, formally or informally, are facing the question of accountability. Accountability, as it applies to principals, very simply refers to how successful a principal is in having his school, its students, staff, and plant achieve a set of agreed-upon goals within a fixed time limit. While it is healthy that school boards are pressing for accountability at all levels of school staff structures, it would be much better if the initiative for effective accountability were taken by principals during their negotiations with school boards rather than the reverse.

The concept of management by objectives or the appraisal of competence in terms of concrete observable achievements is not a new one in the world of business and industry. It is relatively new in education, however. Unfortunately, too many educators—teachers and administrators alike—become alarmed and feel threatened that they are to be judged by the quantity and quality of their productivity—namely, the educational achievements of their students.

Principals should welcome the introduction of accountability requirements. They should include a demand for accountability in their proposals at the bargaining table. The reasons are not hard to understand.

Statement of Duties

Every negotiated agreement should carry a specific list of the responsibilities, functions, and duties of the principal. In hundreds of school districts, no such list has ever been promulgated by board fiat or by joint agreement between principals and boards or superintendents. As a result, too much or too little is expected from the principal—usually, too much. If principals are to be accountable for their performance, they have a right to know what is expected from them and what they should expect from themselves. Moreover, in their negotiations, they should re-examine such lists in order to maintain, reduce, or expand the roster of their functions, as may be meaningful and productive.

Responsibilities Necessitate Authority. If principals negotiate a statement of their duties and responsibilities in their contractual collective covenants with their school boards, they will be in a strong position to insist on a parallel list of powers and prerogatives essential to the fulfillment of the agreed-upon obligations. To require a principal to organize his staff to render the most effective program of instruction must carry with it the power to assign staff according to his best judgment.

Moreover, having once agreed upon this principle, the reduction or elimination of this power cannot be rightfully made in a third party intervention and without prior consultation and renegotiation with the principals' bargaining unit. Should one of the duties of the principal include a provision for orienting a per diem substitute regarding the class work of the absent teacher, he must have the power to direct teachers to prepare materials for use in such orientation.

A board that negotiates away such power by agreeing with teachers to a settlement that they do not have to submit written outlines of projected class activities makes it impractical for the principal to carry out his function and unfair to hold him accountable. This concept must be made very clear when principals bargain with school boards.

Accountability Tools Required. If principals are to be held accountable for the accomplishment of their functions, then they will:

a. Have to be given more voice in the selection of staff members assigned to the school. Many principals, especially in larger school systems, have little or no say in choosing new or replacement members of their school staff—a function often performed solely and entirely by the central office. The accountable principal, who knows his student body and the cultural backgrounds of his school's community, knows that certain types of personality and teaching styles are best suited to his school. His experience is wasted and his achievement of goals is impaired when he is not consulted regarding staff choice.

b. Have to be assured of more prompt responses to their requisitions for building maintenance and repair.

c. Have to be assured of delivery of teaching supplies, texts, audio-visual materials, etc., rather than being forced to operate in short supply.

d. Have to have fully available the special staff needed to render prompt service to special students in terms of diagnosis and treatment rather than having to wait while they suffer and possibly inflict difficulties upon the rest of the school by way of socially negative behavior.

e. Have to have greater input in determining the budgetary needs of the school.

f. Have to be given the authority for more rapid and expeditious handling of staff members whose services are not satisfactory.

g. Have to have available enough administrative assistance to permit their concentration on the attainment of substantive educational objectives.

The Administrative or Management Team

After all is said and done, principals who want to contribute their best to their schools must have real, regular, direct, and meaningful participation in determining the policies by which their school system is managed. There is no question that, in our American democracy, the system of public education belongs to the people and operates under policies determined by the people through their representatives in state legislatures and on school boards. Professional educators would make a serious error if, at any point, they deluded themselves into believing that the people gave them the sole control of educational policy.

School boards employ professionals to conduct the educational process, and they should be able to expect some of them to provide the counsel, guidance, and ideas that board members need in determining policy. Best suited are those that school boards have placed in key positions of leadership and responsibility because of their training, experience, leadership, and record of service to education.

First and foremost among these is the superintendent who, in effect, is a non-voting member of the school board. To carry out his role as the chief policy adviser to the board, forward-looking superintendents in recent years have set up management or administrative teams. In small school districts, these teams have included all principals. In large districts they have included representatives selected by principals' associations along with representatives selected by other associations of supervisors and administrators.

Administrative teams have had some highly desirable results. They have kept the superintendent alerted to the needs for change and to the effects of all existing policies and practices. They have improved morale by giving principals and supervisory staff a higher status. They have given principals an effective channel for contributing to the leadership of their schools. The work of such teams has brought principals closer to negotiations with teachers, custodians, clerks, cafeteria workers, and others so that principals can advise boards and superintendents about the effects certain bargaining demands will have on the schools.

Principals are able to affect and help promulgate policies dealing with budget priorities, school rescheduling, athletic programs, planning of school plant construction, setting up of needed in-service programs, calendar reform, and many more areas. Simultaneously, their contributions have brought about a greater recognition of their potential and an increased confidence in the maintenance and extension of their administrative authority.

With such positive promises for better school administration, the question might well be asked about why management teams have not developed more universally. The major reason is that they usually function at the exclusive determination of the superintendent. When superintendents change, the teams are often not reconstituted. In other cases, the superintendent may become so involved that meetings of the management team become infrequent and insignificant. Some superintendents, of course, are not prepared to consult or share authority because they want things done their way or because they lack confidence in their principals' ability to shape school system policies.

When principals negotiate with boards for guarantees ensuring their status and welfare, they should seek the establishment of an administrative team that will function on mutually agreed-upon standards and will not be determined by one personality. Many school boards and superintendents may need convincing; this becomes a job for negotiators who represent principals at the bargaining table.

VII. *Some Concluding Thoughts*

If superintendents and school boards do not have confidence in their principals, if principals find their powers and prerogatives in a state of erosion, if principals are victims of a sense of insecurity, if the status of principals is far less than it should be as a persuasive force in American education, principals may have themselves to blame.

Principals in the last decade have too often defended their welfare and status, not providing enough leadership in designing and implementing models of change. Some principals may have been too preoccupied with athletic eligibility rules and tournament schedules than with the fact that some students graduate from urban high schools inadequately trained and poorly educated. They have dedicated intense efforts to obtaining accreditation from regional associations rather than examining whether the very criteria for such accreditation are valid or relevant to the education of their students. If principals want better salaries, greater job security, and stated protections of their status, they can achieve them by means of formalized group action. They don't have numbers, it is true, but they do have recognition as leaders of educational improvement, initiators of needed change, and driving forces dedicated to the educational achievement of their students.

Principals who are considering unions should keep in mind that school boards and the public they serve may believe that such a step is oriented to self-serving goals rather than educational leadership. Principals should remember that a major goal of the labor movement is the protection of its workers from the excesses of management—not the protection of one sector of management from another. Actually, they hold a tiger by the tail.

Professional associations will have to begin to think about doing more than reacting to major educational issues. They will have to be the initiators of ideas and processes in education to which others react. They will have to begin to become the think-tank organizations that champion educational experiment. Closer to the daily reality of problems facing young people and their schools, principals as an organized force must buttonhole legislators, meet with superintendents, develop liaison with school board associations, establish rapport with business and labor, and work closely with the spokesmen of minorities.

For what purpose? Primarily to deal with educational inadequacies and with strategies to provide for the unmet needs of youth. How to prepare teachers better; how to develop programs for young people that will be far more productive and satisfying to young people than the culture of drugs and the occult; how to overcome the disease of racial hatred among their students; how to encourage creative talent; how to reorganize schools to serve individuals rather than masses; and how to build structures to enlist the creativity of youth for human betterment rather than to overcome boredom and disillusion.

These are the tasks that must become priority activities of the local and state associations of principals. Principals' associations will have little to worry about in terms of "muscle" or "clout" at any bargaining table if they have won their stripes as spokesmen and fighters for providing young people the finest kind of education. Their influence will precede them.

Related NASSP Publications

Legal Memoranda

The Legal Status of the Principal, Revised. 1973.

The Administrator's Right to Continuing Employment. 1973.

Special Publications

Employment Contracts for Secondary School Administrators. Presents trends in secondary administrator employment contracts. Includes definitions, contract analyses by state, and sample contracts. 1974.

Administering a Negotiated Contract. Sets forth new formulas for administering schools under master contracts. 1973.

Administrative Appraisal: A Step to Improved Leadership. Emphasizes involvement of the administrative team in developing an evaluation program. 1972.

Management Crisis: A Solution. Shows how well-organized administrative teams can ensure maximum involvement of the principal in school district policy making. 1971.

What is Negotiable? First in the NASSP pamphlet series dealing with issues in professional negotiations from the principal's viewpoint. Benjamin Epstein presents six criteria for deciding what to include and what to exclude from the negotiations process. 1969.

Principals and Grievance Procedures. In this second pamphlet in NASSP's PN series, Louis Kramer examines the need for carefully-worked-out procedures

40

for handling grievances. He also gives examples of good grievance procedures, with emphasis on important features, along with advice to principals on administering them. 1969.

Critical Issues in Negotiations Legislation. R. L. Ackerly and W. S. Johnson review eight issues to be considered in designing negotiations legislation. 1969.

The Principal's Role in Collective Negotiations Between Teachers and School Boards. Discussion of principals' status in the changing relationships among teachers, administrators, and school boards. 1965.

The Principalship: Job Specifications and Salary Considerations for the 70's. Discussion of up-dated criteria intended to more precisely define the modern role of the principal. Other major sections include a new statement of principals' salaries and suggestions concerning how to evaluate performance. Appendix lists data on administrative salaries from 34 selected school districts. 1970.

The Assistant Principalship. Report of a national study on the assistant principalship as revealed by a shadow study, a review of career-development patterns, and a wide variety of other data relating to the position and the people who hold it. 1970.

The Senior High-School Principalship. Results of a comprehensive survey of the backgrounds, present positions, school programs, and professional opinions of more than 16,000 high school principals. 1965.

The Junior High-School Principalship. Results of a comprehensive survey of the backgrounds, present positions, school programs, and professional opinions of some 4,500 junior-high principals. 1966.